P9-EEN-854

Hamilton, Sue L.
Arnold Schwarzenegger

REACHING FOR THE STARS

ARNOLD SCHWARZENEGGER
NO. 1 MOVIE STAR IN THE WORLD

Written By: Sue L. Hamilton

Published by Abdo & Daughters, 6535 Cecilia Circle, Edina, Minnesota 55439.

Library bound edition distributed by Rockbottom Books, Pentagon Tower, P.O. Box 36036, Minneapolis, Minnesota 55435.

Printed in the United States.

Cover Photo: Retna, LTD
Inside Photos: Globe Photos 4, 7, 9, 10, 15, 17, 19, 21, 22, 25, 26, 28 & 30

Edited by John Hamilton

LIBRARY OF CONGRESS CATALOGING-IN-PUBLICATION DATA

Hamilton, Sue L., 1959-
   Arnold Schwarzenegger / written by Sue Hamilton.
      p. cm. — (Reaching for the Stars)
   Summary: Examines the career of the Austrian-born bodybuilder who became an enormous box-office success in a second career as a movie star.
   ISBN 1-56239-144-5
   1. Schwarzenegger, Arnold -- Juvenile literature. 2. Bodybuilders -- Austria -- Biography -- Juvenile literature. 3. Bodybuilders -- United States -- Biography -- Juvenile literature. 4. Motion picture actors and actresses -- United States -- Biography -- Juvenile literature. [1. Schwarzenegger, Arnold. 2. Bodybuilders. 3. Actors and actresses.] I. Title. II. Series.
GV545.52S38H36 1992   646.7'5'092--dc20   92-16035
                                              [B]

International Standard Book Number:	Library of Congress Catalog Card Number:
1-56239-144-5	92-16035

TABLE OF CONTENTS

Arnold Schwarzenegger: Big man with big ambitions.

ARNOLD

"Someday the world is going to know who I am—just by hearing my first name, Arnold," said Arnold Schwarzenegger to movie studio professionals, as he began his film career in the mid-1970's. Many people advised him to take on the name "Arnold Strong," and he did do his first movie, *Hercules Goes Bananas*, in 1970 under that name. But Arnold, a big man with a big name and big plans for success, believed in himself and determinedly kept his name and stuck to his own plans for fame and fortune.

Today, Schwarzenegger (meaning "black plowman") is a name known worldwide. States Tom Pollock, Chairman of Universal Pictures, "Arnold Schwarzenegger is a movie star throughout the world: the United States, England, Continental Europe, the Middle East, Asia. There is no place, right now, that he is not a star."

From his teenage years growing up in Austria and turning to the sport of bodybuilding, Arnold has always wanted to be on top. Not surprisingly, his determination and will to succeed have made him just that: Number 1.

GROWING UP IN AUSTRIA

Arnold was born July 30, 1947 in the small village of Thal, Austria. His father, Gustav Schwarzenegger, was police chief of the village. His mother, Aurelia, was an excellent homemaker, always keeping their home immaculately clean, as well as sewing clothes and finding time to bake.

Arnold was their second son. Meinhard, Arnold's older brother, had been born almost exactly one year earlier on July 17, 1946.

Growing up with a father as police chief, especially when one is a prankster, wasn't always easy for the young Arnold or his older brother. In the documentary movie *Pumping Iron*, Arnold says, "We had to be the perfect example; we couldn't do anything bad. And it was kind of an uptight feeling at home because of it."

Gustav Schwarzenegger's salary, although always regular, did not lend itself to extravagance. Meat was a special treat for Sunday dinner. They had no television, and Arnold distinctly remembers the excitement of receiving the family's first refrigerator.

Both boys were good athletes. From their earliest days, the Schwarzenegger brothers often competed with each other to see who was "best."

Although Arnold was part of a soccer team in his early teens, he found that he really preferred "competing" against himself. And to that end, the 14-year-old Arnold traveled to the nearby town of Graz to begin his weightlifting career.

Arnold getting serious.

PUMPING IRON

Arnold began "pumping iron" at age 14 at the Graz
Athletic Union, a club of weightlifters. Although already
6'2" tall, Arnold walked into the Union with, as one
trainer there has said, "very bad posture, a slightly
shrunken chest, fallen shoulders, and very skinny legs."
Most of the older weightlifters found him too smug. After
having trained only a short time, he announced, "Well, I
give myself about five years and I will be Mr. Universe."
(In fact, it took him six years.)

Meinhard Schwarzenegger also gave a half-hearted at-
tempt at weightlifting. He joined his brother Arnold at the
Union for a few sessions. Although Meinhard had the
better physical build (muscular with small hips), he did
not have Arnold's determination. Bored, Meinhard quit.
Dedicated, Arnold continued. His persistence soon earned
him the grudging admiration of the other weightlifters.

The young Arnold watched and learned many tricks.
During the early 1960's, it was common practice for
weightlifters to use steroids. Today, Arnold does not use
them. Their dangerous effects can include cancer, liver
damage and failure, high blood pressure, damage to the
heart, and damage to the reproductive system. However,
back in 1961, Arnold never thought twice about following
the ways of the Austrian bodybuilding community. Natu-
rally, his constant training and steroids had a dramatic
effect on the young Austrian's body.

On October 30, 1965, just months after turning 18, Arnold won his first international competition: the Jr. Mr. Europe in Stuttgaard, Germany. At this time he was in the Austrian army for his required one-year of service. In order to compete, he had to go AWOL (away without leave). He returned to his station just outside of Graz, and spent seven days in jail. However, word of his victory in Stuttgaard spread quickly, and after his punishment was completed, he was encouraged to work out even harder to win more contests and better Austria's image.

Arnold has been Mr. Universe 5 times and Mr. Olympia 7.

Even Gustav and Aurelia Schwarzenegger, who had never really liked their son taking part in this "sport," were impressed with Arnold's win and his trophy. They announced proudly to friends and strangers alike, "That's my son." Still, they encouraged Arnold to make bodybuilding a part-time sport, and pursue a career either in the military or continue with carpentry, an occupation he had begun in order to make money while bodybuilding.

However, for Arnold, part-time was not enough. He wanted to be "the greatest bodybuilder in the world, the greatest bodybuilder of all time."

In 1967, Arnold was well on his way to becoming "the greatest." That year he became the youngest man ever to win the Mr. Universe title, competing in London at the National Amateur Body Builders Association (NABBA). At the time, he was 20 years old, stood 6'2" tall, weighed 235 pounds, had 22" arms, 28 1/2" thighs, 20" calves, a 34" waist and a 57" chest. The following year, he won the title again. Clearly, he had succeeded in Europe. Now it was time to move on.

Arnold well on his way to becoming the greatest bodybuilder ever.

MOVING TO AMERICA

"I always felt that my place was in America," stated Arnold. "And when I was 10 years old I only dreamed of coming to America and being the greatest. And just being different from everybody else." His dream came true in September 1968.

Arnold arrived in Miami with one gym bag of clothing. At the last minute, he had been invited by Joe Weider, president of the worldwide professional bodybuilding organization, to compete at the International Federation of Body Builders (IFBB).

Arnold's first competition, only 24 hours after arriving, was less than successful. Pale, tired, and used to competing for a different audience, Arnold lost to Frank Zane, recent winner of the Mr. America contest.

Despite the loss, Joe Weider saw in Arnold great opportunities, and offered him a "job." In exchange for his plane fare to the United States and a small weekly salary, Arnold would lend his name and body to advertise any products that Joe asked him to. Here was Arnold's chance to stay in America and train. Arnold agreed and signed the contract.

Although it was a great break, it was nevertheless a rough time for the young Austrian. "I could not speak the language well at all. I couldn't listen to the news.

I couldn't read the papers... It was the most difficult time in my life," said Arnold years later.

Of course, Arnold did not quit. "Strength does not come from winning. Your struggles develop your strengths. When you go through hardships and decide not to surrender, that is strength..." Arnold built great strength in those next months—both physically and mentally. He spent hours in the gym, but he also spent hours learning. Although still struggling with English, Arnold enrolled in the University of Wisconsin, and graduated with a degree in business. Why business? Says Arnold, "Unless you know what to do with your money, it doesn't do you any good to make it."

In the late 1960's and early 1970's, Gold's Gym in Santa Monica, California was the center of bodybuilding. Most serious bodybuilders trained there. It was no surprise that Arnold also ended up there. He trained six days a week, four plus hours a day. He loved the warmth of the California sun, and quickly took to the freedom and independence America offered.

The years became a blur of training, dating girls, competing and winning. "We all have great inner power. The power is self-faith. There's really an attitude to winning. You have to see yourself winning before you win. And you have to be hungry. You have to want to conquer." Arnold won... time after time.

1970 brought him to a new challenge: movie-making. Arnold began his career in the made-for-Italian-television movie called, *Hercules Goes to New York* (also known as *Hercules Goes Bananas*). Because of his heavy accent, Arnold's voice was dubbed over by another actor's voice. It was a less-than-glorious beginning, with Arnold acting under the name "Arnold Strong." Still, it gave him a taste for his future.

1970 became the year 23-year-old Arnold achieved bodybuilding's triple crown. He again won the NABBA Mr. Universe London. Two days later and halfway around the world, he won the Pro Mr. World contest in Columbus, Ohio. Two weeks after that, Arnold took first place in the Mr. Olympia competition in New York.

As the years passed, Arnold became the undisputed king of bodybuilding, winning contest after contest. However, the early 1970's also saw personal tragedies for Arnold. First, his brother, Meinhard, while driving drunk, ran into another car and was killed instantly on May 20, 1971. Then, less than two years later, on December 11, 1972, Arnold's father, Gustav, died of a stroke.

As the years passed, Arnold found he needed a new challenge...

"CONAN" THE CAREER MAKER

"I can zero in on a vision of where I want to be in the future. I can see it so clearly in front of me when I daydream that it's almost a reality. Then I get this easy feeling, and I don't have to be uptight to get there because I already feel like I'm there, that it's just a matter of time."

Arnold Schwarzenegger wanted to be a movie star. "I made up a program. Went to a lot of acting classes, voice classes, accent-removal classes, and on and on... And then I met the most incredible resistance that you can imagine." Because there had been no one like him before—a foreign-born, heavily-accented bodybuilder—many in Hollywood thought his chances of succeeding were slim. However, once again, Arnold gained strength through defeat and doggedly continued his goal.

And of course there was the problem with his name. Schwarzenegger recalled one meeting with an agent: "'I tell you, your name won't sell. I cannot pronounce it,' he said, 'and no one else can in this office, right girls?' And they all laughed. 'Yeah, Schwarzenschnitzel or what's the name here... You have to change your name or do something with it.' And so I said to myself, oh, here, another beating."

"Conan the Barbarian."

Still, Arnold persisted and earned a role playing an owner of a workout club in the 1975 film, *Stay Hungry* with Sally Field and Jeff Bridges. He surprised many people with his abilities, including a part where he had to pretend to "play the fiddle." He studied how it was done, and when the filming was going on, several people watching commented about how "that big fella can really play."

In late 1975, Arnold became the center of the documentary-style film, *Pumping Iron*, whereupon he announced his retirement: "Bodybuilding has been a beautiful experience for me and I will continue it for the rest of my life. I'm only stopping competing bodybuilding, but I'm not stopping bodybuilding. Thank you..." For Schwarzenegger, six-time Mr. Olympia and five-time Mr. Universe, a new time had come.

1979 brought him the opportunity to become "the handsome stranger" in the western comedy, *The Villain*. Although he had doubts about the film—it did very poorly, with reviewers comparing Arnold's acting to that of his horse—he enjoyed the opportunity to work with movie greats Ann-Margaret and Kirk Douglas.

Next came his 1980 TV movie, *The Jayne Mansfield Story*. Arnold portrayed 1950's movie star Jayne Mansfield's (played by Loni Anderson) bodybuilder husband, Mickey Hargitay. In real life, Hargitay had won the NABBA Mr. Universe title in 1956—11 years before Arnold would win it himself.

Meantime, the frantically busy Schwarzenegger was working as a CBS commentator for bodybuilding events. With only a few weeks of training, he came out of bodybuilding retirement to compete in the 1980 Mr. Olympia. Filmed as part of *The Comeback*, Arnold won the competition. Some members of the audience, who had their own favorites, loudly complained of the judges' choice, booing

Arnold uses ballet to refine his routine.

and throwing things. Nevertheless, Schwarzenegger walked away as a seven-time winner of the Mr. Olympia title.

It was the 1982 film *Conan the Barbarian* that gave Arnold his first starring role. Arnold was the spitting image of Robert E. Howard's comic-strip super-hero "Conan." Filming was no easy task. They started out in below-zero temperatures and ended up in sweltering heat surrounded by waves of hungry mosquitoes.

With director John Milius' vision for the movie, Arnold performed all his own stunts. "John wants to bring to the screen as much reality as possible. If you're attacked by a vulture, he wants a real vulture. If you fight with broadswords, he wants real swords that weigh 10 pounds.

Which, of course, puts you in danger as an actor." During the filming, Arnold was attacked by live wolves, 20 horses, and amateur sword-wielding actors, causing him several trips to the doctor for stitches and medication. Yet, with John Milius's clear direction and Arnold's own confidence and powerful body, *Conan* was released in the United States on May 14, 1982. It became the top summer movie and went on to earn $100 million worldwide. Arnold was suddenly a star.

On September 16, 1983, Arnold became an American citizen, announcing, "When I came here to America, it was like heaven... All the great things have happened to me since I came here." One great thing was meeting his future bride, Maria Shriver, niece of the late President John F. Kennedy, and successful news journalist in her own right. They first met back in 1977 at a Robert F. Kennedy Tennis Tournament. Throughout the next six years, they dated long distance, meeting at either Maria's East Coast home or Arnold's place in California, and were finally married on April 16, 1986.

Shortly after receiving his citizenship, Arnold began filming *Conan the Destroyer*. It opened in July 1984 to less-than-outstanding reviews. However, it did well at the box office. Already Arnold was bringing people to the movies by his name alone.

Arnold with actress Grace Jones in "Conan the Destroyer."

"THE TERMINATOR"

If the *Conan* movies made him a star, *The Terminator* made him a superstar. Using exactly 17 lines of dialog (65 words), the actor turned the 1984 movie, and himself, into a hit. Arnold played a cyborg from the future, sent back to the 1980's to terminate the woman Sarah Connor (played by Linda Hamilton). Sarah's yet-unborn son, John, would be leader of those trying to destroy the cyborgs in the year 2029.

Directed by James Cameron (*Aliens*), the story, action, and acting all made Arnold famous, and set a precedent for how people would define "Schwarzenegger" movies: exciting, full of special effects and stunts, at times funny, and most of all, entertaining. And of course, his famous movie one-liner, "I'll be back," would become his signature line.

Throughout the 1980's, Schwarzenegger would make movie after movie. With few exceptions, all were box office hits:

Commando	1985
Red Sonja	1985
Raw Deal	1986
Predator	1987
The Running Man	1987
Red Heat	1988

"The Terminator."

These pictures showed Arnold in many different roles, but always the leading fighter, the man with muscles and brains. Arnold, now in his early 40's, decided he wanted something a bit different in his next role.

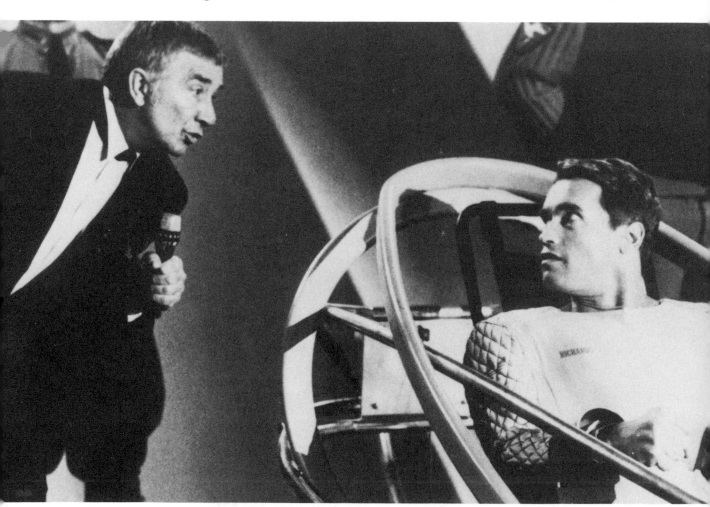

Arnold with actor Richard Dawson in "The Running Man."

HAVING FUN AND
MAKING FUN

Comedy is often thought of as something for someone like Robin Williams or Steve Martin to do. But is it something for a muscle man? Strangely enough, all through his movies, Arnold had incorporated his own brand of humor—simple puns and one-liners that would make his audience laugh. Some were directed at himself or a movie situation, but they all helped to make people like him even more.

With this approach, Arnold joined with comedic actor Danny DeVito to make the 1988 movie, *Twins*. Here, tall, muscle-bound Julius (Arnold) is twin brother to short, struggling Vincent (DeVito). The two twin brothers, separated at birth, meet for the first time and go in search of their mother. It's a fun film, as DeVito teaches the less street-smart Arnold all the ways of the world. Audiences loved this new look at their favorite actor.

On the heels of the success of his first comedy came the success of another title—that of dad. Arnold and Maria welcomed their first daughter, Katherine Eunice Schwarzenegger, into the world on December 13, 1989.

Arnold soon went on to another type of film—a science-fiction type movie called *Total Recall*. Arnold's character travels to Mars to save the planet, and must figure out whether he's in fact a good or bad guy. Throughout the movie, one is never exactly sure who to trust, but somehow Arnold stays on the edge, rapidly gaining audience support for the likable, yet confused, rescuer. As has become his trademark, this film provides movie-goers with the trademark action/special effects expected of a Schwarzenegger picture. It took in an amazing $262 million worldwide box office. And as Peter Hoffman, President of Carolco Pictures (the distributors of the movie) points out, "...you have to look to Arnold as the principle source of its monstrous success."

1990 brought Arnold back to comedy, with the popular *Kindergarten Cop*. As a tough Los Angeles police officer, Arnold's character must travel to the small town of Astoria, Oregon, where he takes on the role of kindergarten teacher while doing an undercover drug investigation on one of the kid's parents. The muscular policeman is scared stiff of the small-fry. However, using his cop approach, he once again succeeds not only in handling the killer drug dealer, but the kindergarteners as well. Not a surprise to anyone, the film became a major success.

During all these successes, Arnold also entered the world of politics. President Bush, whom Arnold actively campaigned for, dubbed Schwarzenegger, "Conan the Republican." Although Arnold could never run for president (a president must be American-born), he does not deny that politics strongly interest him. One day, he may even run for a position such as Senator or Governor.

Arnold surrounded by young costars in "Kindergarten Cop."

Arnold's back in "Terminator 2: Judgment Day."

HOW TO EARN $12 MILLION

The first *Terminator* movie was shot in 48 days on a $6.4 million budget and earned $100 million in worldwide ticket sales. The sequel, *Terminator 2: Judgment Day* was shot in 6 months, cost an estimated $94 million, and has earned $490 million in worldwide ticket sales.

How did the $94 million break out?

- *$12 million*: Schwarzenegger's salary (the bulk of which was reportedly taken in the form of a Gulfstream III jet)
- *$6 million:* James Cameron's salary as producer/director/co-writer
- *$10 million:* Rights to make the sequel
- *$1 million:* Linda Hamilton's salary
- *$4 million:* Other prefilming costs, including actors' salaries
- *$17 million:* Special effects
- *$34 million:* Other production costs from stunts to catering
- *$10 million:* Interest and overhead

_____

$94 million/TOTAL

In *T2*, the T800 (Arnold) switches to the "good guy" role, having been sent back in time to protect 10-year-old John Connor (played by newcomer Edward Furlong), from the new, more sophisticated terminator model, the T1000 (played by Robert Patrick).

Arnold with wife Maria Shriver touring London.

Made of liquid metal, the T1000 can mold itself into the shape of any person or thing.

The $94 million budget was unbelievable. Never before had a picture cost so much. Around the world, people wondered what they would see. They got what they paid for (both the movie studio and the audiences)!

The special effects for the T1000 were state-of-the-art. The stunts — fantastic. The action — riveting. The result? A blockbuster hit with the Number 1 movie star in the world—Arnold Schwarzenegger.

People's Choice winner.

"I'll BE BACK"

"Good things don't happen by coincidence... Every dream carries with it certain risks, especially the risk of failure. But I am not stopped by risks. Suppose a person takes the risk and fails. Then the person must try again. You cannot fail forever. If you try ten times, you have a better chance of making it on the eleventh try than if you didn't try at all."

Arnold has tried. He has seen failure. Now he sees unbelievable success. Only weeks after *T2* broke box office sales records, Arnold and Maria welcomed their second daughter into the world on July 24, 1991. As head of the President's Council on Physical Fitness, Arnold continues to promote the benefits of sports. He, himself, still finds time between being a husband, father, and movie star, to work out at least an hour a day.

We know that as the years pass, in whatever type of role—be it action/adventure, science fiction, comedy, musical (yes, even that's been thought of!), or as a director, politician, or fitness expert—Arnold Schwarzenegger will continue to say:

"I'll be back."

"I'll be back."